STARTING YOUR OWN ~~SIDE HUSTLE~~ MICROBUSINESS

LAUNCH A SCALABLE BUSINESS ON THE SIDE

Weston Seid

Khiry Kemp

Print ISBN: 978-1-54398-414-9
eBook ISBN: 978-1-54398-415-6

TABLE OF CONTENTS

PART I:
INTRODUCTION

"The first step towards getting somewhere is to decide you're not going to stay where you are."

— John Pierpont "J.P." Morgan

Warren Buffett. Everyone knows Warren Buffett. He's considered to be one of the most successful business magnates of all-time. He's the CEO of Berkshire Hathaway, the fifth largest company in the world at the time of this writing. But when and how did he start? Before he accumulated a personal fortune worth billions of dollars, Buffett had been engaged in operating much smaller businesses and learning as much as he could. He also says that he "peaked very early" in his business career. How early? At seventeen-years-old.

Born in 1930, it would take only six years before Buffett would begin making profit by selling gum in packs of five to his neighbors. He was charging five cents per pack, and quickly upgraded to selling Coca-Cola because there was an opportunity to make more money. Business experience can come at any age, and the amazing thing about it is that it compounds continuously providing lessons to learn from and improve. A few years later, Buffett was experiencing success as a paperboy, and even identified ways to sell calendars and magazine subscriptions to his newspaper customer base. Then, he established his first company, Buffett's Used Golf Balls, which would buy refurbished golf balls from a different market, and sell them locally for almost twice the price. He would go on to create ventures by selling stamps and washing cars, all before age seventeen.

With each experience preparing him for the next, Buffett was refining his business sense and ability to identify and explore solid opportunities. By age seventeen, he identified an opportunity to make an investment and earn passive income. Until this venture, all his business experiences were labor intensive. His new idea would enable Buffett to invest money upfront and earn continuous income without actually being present for sales to customers. He bought a pinball machine, had a friend fix it up, and then made a deal with a local barbershop to position the machine for men to play while waiting for their haircuts. After pitching his idea to the barber, there was an agreement made in which Buffett would split the profits 50/50. A week later, Buffett made enough money to cover the cost of the pinball machine, and he immediately bought another machine. Before long, he had built an empire of eight pinball machines around his town, which enabled him to sustainably earn money without physically being at the barbershops. This pinball operation became what he would describe as his "best business ever."

When people invest their money, they generally expect to receive annual returns of 3–11 percent, but Buffett was able to earn 100 percent of his pinball investment in just a week. He had a scalable business, with an initial investment that could be recovered completely in seven days. The business would continue to grow as long as the people in barbershops continued to play pinball. Also, everybody benefited. The people waiting for haircuts had an entertaining game to play while waiting, the barbers made additional revenue, and Buffett earned money because he identified an opportunity and executed his idea.

From golf balls to pinball machines, Buffett engaged in **microbusinesses** that were executable within his means, and experimental in ways to develop first-hand experience. As we see from his example, it's never too early to start.

Now you must be asking, "What in the world is a 'microbusiness'?" "Is it the same as a 'side hustle'?" Our answer: Not really. We define a side hustle as a part-time, labor-based operation, in which the primary focus is to earn immediate income, without the intent to scale or create passive income. An example of a side hustle is when someone is driving part-time for a rideshare company to earn extra income, and is receiving compensation only by driving passengers to their destinations.

Comparatively, a microbusiness is more strategic and usually has longer term considerations in the approach. Over the years, we've come to define a microbusiness as an organization consisting of one or two core founders who initiate transactions or exchanges based on four primary intentions:

- Establish passive income
- Improve lifestyle access and experience
- Validate a business model or management ability
- Create community impact

To make the distinction between a side hustle and a microbusiness, it is absolutely critical to understand the founder's intentions.

Even if an individual only has one of these primary intentions, their operation would still qualify as a microbusiness. A founder may have several reasons to create a business operation, but we specify "primary intent" because there is usually a motivational force that is more prevalent than the rest. For example, someone may feel the need to create community impact more than they want to establish passive income.

Among the four primary intentions, most people launch microbusinesses to create passive income. The idea of creating a sustainable source of income that almost maintains itself is attractive to many. Those that are starting a business to establish passive income may have to perform upfront labor, but they're working to create a system that could sustainably generate revenue without a huge time commitment. If your intent is to establish passive income, you may consider renting out something you own, or creating an information product like an online course or tutorial.

You can also create a microbusiness with the primary intention of improving your lifestyle access and experience. People do this to obtain an otherwise out-of-reach asset, or to directly secure access to a desired experience, product, or service. For example, if you establish a popular social media page or blog for the main purpose of having restaurants offer you free meals in exchange for food reviews, this is improving your lifestyle and giving you access to meals that you would've otherwise had to pay for.

If your primary intention of starting a business is to validate a business model or your own management ability, this also qualifies as a microbusiness. To test the viability of a particular idea, you may be laying the foundation for a startup company by interacting with potential customers to gauge interest in early versions of your future product. Some young people create microbusinesses primarily to measure their own abilities to manage a small operation and gain leadership experience along the way. This is usually carried out when there's an active effort to improve their entrepreneurial skillset, and the founder genuinely wants to practice management to prepare for having larger teams and higher-stake scenarios in the future.

Lastly, if you're creating an organization with the primary purpose of helping the community, this would be a microbusiness because you'll most likely manage other members to help you accomplish your goals over a long period of time, and your actions wouldn't be driven by short-term revenue generation. This is definitely not a side hustle. Remember, side hustles focus on making immediate profit via labor-based, part-time work.

From our definition, you can see that many businesses exist without the primary intent of earning profit. If you want to start a microbusiness to receive donated clothing and gift the items to people in need, it's not mandatory for you to profit from this exchange. It's completely up to you to determine how much profit you would need to receive to make the effort worth your time. This microbusiness could forego profit completely, and still successfully work towards its social improvement.

If a company is established primarily to create and promote social benefit, it might be eligible to receive 501(c)(3) status by the Internal Revenue Service (IRS) to be officially recognized as a non-profit company, which means that it must explicitly state that the earnings will not be used for the personal gain or benefits of its founders, employees, supporters, relatives, or associates. The government supports these businesses, and as an additional business incentive, these organizations can receive tax-deductible donations from individuals and businesses. They are not taxed on earned revenue.

Causes that fit within the IRS's approval criteria include:

- Charity
- Cruelty Prevention
- Education
- Literary
- Public Safety
- Religion
- Science

Examples of non-profit organizations include: hospitals, universities, national charities, churches, and foundations. Even though it's very difficult to start a new hospital, there are many young people that create microbusiness charities and foundations to launch their entrepreneurial journeys.

Often, young people begin their entrepreneurial paths based on a particular set of skills that they've developed over time. With just a small nudge to pursue their curiosity, they regularly choose to create microbusinesses out of teaching others how to improve their abilities. For example, if you're really great at Math, and a classmate offers to pay you for private tutoring, you could have a side hustle if you trained that one classmate with the purpose of earning immediate revenue, but you could have a microbusiness if you created online tutorials that could generate revenue whenever people watched your content. Either way, you'd be able to earn money by doing something that you're already good at, but by thinking ahead, you can look for opportunities to scale. If you're doing one-on-one tutoring sessions, your upper limit of daily sessions is the number of hours you have in a day, but the online tutorial method can reach thousands of students before you even get out of bed in the morning.

Fundamentally, microbusinesses should run very lean in terms of scale and headcount, and successful founders are able to find efficient ways to stretch limited resources. For product-based businesses, it is important to minimize inventory costs, meaning that you should not have an abundance of products collecting dust while waiting to be sold. However, technological advances have now made it possible to sell products via "drop-shipping," a process where a person or business can make a sale of a product not within their possession, buy the item from a third-party, and have it shipped directly to the customer. This is very lean because the person or business has the benefit of not having to store inventory.

We've described that a side hustle can transition into a microbusiness if the primary intention of the founder changes, but what does a microbusiness progress into? Based on scale and overall growth, a microbusiness can directly transition to become a startup company or a small business with up to 500 employees, according to the Small Business Administration (SBA). If a microbusiness progresses to the startup or small business phase, the founders usually engage in full-time work efforts to stimulate continued development and success. Also, a microbusiness can continue to operate as a microbusiness, and once it reaches a sustainable state, it doesn't necessarily have to scale any further.

In the chapters that follow, we walk you through several microbusiness case studies to show how an idea goes from initiation to business success, and we provide a guide for you to launch your own microbusiness. We highlight intentions and actions to show the importance of strategy and how it impacts the way a microbusiness develops over time.

PART II:
MICROBUSINESS
CASE STUDIES

OVERVIEW

"Listen. Take the best. Leave the rest."

-Richard Branson

Now that you have a foundational understanding of the microbusiness concept, we'll provide you with several examples that walk you through the detailed steps that were taken to execute various business ideas. These examples explore the journey of microbusinesses created by young entrepreneurs, and we've captured their stories in the pages that follow. All the following microbusinesses were created on a part-time schedule, by young people who were interested in starting a business, and were bold enough to take action. While reading these case studies, pay attention to the origin of the idea and the initial planning that took place. By providing a range of examples, it is our hope that you find inspiration and knowledge that you can apply toward your entrepreneurial journey. Our goal is not to have you memorize these cases, but rather to find value in the approaches and apply what you can toward your business idea.

Case Study #1: Tesloop

"You want to be in the driver's seat of your own life, because if you are not, life will drive you."

-Oprah Winfrey

For many teens, successfully earning a state driver's license is the first step to solidifying coolness and independence. Behind the wheel of a car, you feel empowered, and you've been patiently waiting to drive by yourself without adult supervision. You've seen the *Fast & the Furious* movie franchise, or at least watched with envy as your neighbor or older sibling started driving before you, and now it's your time to shine. Now, the next question is, "What car will you drive? How will you get it?" Some parents predetermine the answer to that question: By the time you've reached driving age, it's already been decided that you will receive either a new vehicle, or a used vehicle from the car lot, or a passed-down vehicle that has already been in the family. However, in some cases, teens can be involved in the conversation, influence the outcome, and obtain parental support for a car they'd prefer to drive.

Haydn Sonnad was finishing up his sophomore year of high school when the time had come for him to start driving. He had passed his driving exam and was looking to finally hit the road in a car of his own. Which car did he want? For him the decision was clear: He wanted a Tesla Model S. You see, Haydn had been reading up on the company and consuming news articles about the car for over a year-and-a-half prior to receiving his driver's license, and he was extremely fascinated by the sophisticated technological capabilities that were never-before seen in a car. It was a gorgeous electric vehicle with the promise of being able to drive itself someday in the future. As a car enthusiast, this was a car that Haydn believed to be a "game-changer," and a truly magnificent creation. Like most teens, Haydn didn't have the luxury of being able to ask his parents to buy the Tesla for him, so he had to get creative if he wanted to turn his dream into reality. Here is where his car-based entrepreneurial journey begins.

The year was 2015. Tesla, the company responsible for manufacturing the stylish "car of the future" and "computer on wheels," had offered free electric charging if customers refueled at one of the Tesla charging stations. Essentially, as an incentive for purchasing, it was like buying a car and having free gas for life. Also, Tesla's CEO, Elon Musk, had implemented a policy called the "Happiness Guarantee" that enabled customers to simply return the car after three months, for any reason, if they were unhappy with the experience. These two details, the free charging and the Happiness Guarantee, would play a significant role in the initial plan that Haydn put together. He started thinking about ways in which he could use the car to generate revenue, and because he didn't have to pay for gas, it occurred to him that he could hypothetically give people rides and keep 100 percent of whatever price he charged the passengers.

This approach is what we described earlier as a "lifestyle" microbusiness, which is when a business enables the founder(s) to reduce personal costs related to enjoying a particular product or service, or to achieve substantial non-financial benefits associated with operating a particular business. In this case, Haydn's personal costs of ownership would be reduced by making shuttle trips, thereby making his desired car more affordable. As a sixteen-year-old, to be able to drive a car that had a retail value of at least $70,000, the successful execution of his microbusiness would grant him the personal enjoyment of being able to attain something otherwise unattainable due to his financial circumstances.

Haydn's dad wasn't exactly supportive of this in the beginning, and even though Haydn told him about the Happiness Guarantee, there were still concerns about safety and regulatory matters. Haydn's dad recommended that Haydn get more validation from people who know a little more about the industry and could advise on the execution of his idea. Haydn took this recommendation quite literally and quickly devised a plan to gain access to the Tesla shareholder meeting, sit close to where the microphones were, and ask the CEO a question during the Q&A session. Haydn had asked Musk about the development of autopilot technology. Specifically, he was thinking about lending his car out to drivers who could pick up passengers and take them to their destinations, and he asked Musk if the autopilot technology could be trusted to keep the passengers and his car intact. The Tesla CEO responded by saying that the early version of autopilot required a driver to be alert and remain ready to resume control, but that in several years, a driver would be able to sleep while autopilot is engaged. This was great news for Haydn because this meant that one day his car could make money by shuttling people without a human driver in the car at all.

Filled with confidence after the shareholder meeting in which he spoke with the CEO, Haydn's confidence was strong and his idea was picking up momentum. To further validate the feasibility of the idea and refine the approach, here are some of the remaining key questions that had he had to address:

- Were there any complications around the operation of a shuttle vehicle for a sixteen-year-old, newly licensed driver in the state of California?
- How much would the Model S cost to operate?
- How much should passengers pay per trip?
- How many rides would he need to break even? How much money could he make during the three month Happiness Guarantee period?
- Which roundtrip routes would be the best to drive? Most popular? Most profitable?

Haydn had just received his license and was aware that it would be difficult to convince anyone that he was qualified to drive them any further than the local supermarket. Also, because it was a formal shuttle service, Haydn found that it would be extremely expensive to insure the car as a sixteen-year-old using the car for commercial purposes. He realized that he wouldn't be able to "pilot" the car himself, but that if he found drivers, he could still enjoy the car when it wasn't being used for the shuttle service. How much would it cost to hire drivers?

Haydn's initial research led him to the following calculations: To lease the car would cost $2000 per month, and the insurance would cost an additional $500 per month. There would be no cost for a driver if he were to drive the car himself, but since he would have to employ drivers, the cost would be $20 per hour multiplied by the number of hours driven during the month. Thinking about a roundtrip route in which he could charge $100 per person and have three passengers each way, he estimated that he could make up to $600 in revenue, each day of operation. If the drivers were to drive six hours per day, then the cost would be $120 per day, and with the promotional free refueling offer that came with the Model S, there were no electricity costs. With a profit of $480 per day of operation, it would take him just over five days to be able to pay his lease and insurance payments, with any additional days of operation leading to net profit.

Expected Daily Revenue – (# of tickets x ticket price)	6 tickets x $100 = $600/day
Expected Daily Cost – (# of hours x driver wage)	6 hours x $20/hr = $120
Expected Daily Profit (Revenue – Cost)	$480
Monthly Car Lease & Insurance Cost	~$2500
Number of Days for the car pay for itself	~5.2 days

Hypothetically, if he could have his car drive every day of the month with the same assumptions, it would be possible for him to earn a profit of $12,000 in the first month, and $36,000 by the end of the third month. Without a doubt, this would be incredibly difficult to pull off, but seeing this sort of potential motivated Haydn to take this opportunity seriously.

To determine the most profitable routes, the benefit of free charging again proved to be an important factor. Haydn determined that the savings generated from not having to pay for fuel would be maximized if the car took long distance trips. Put another way, the more the car was driven, the more money the car saved on fuel costs compared to other vehicles, which again was a unique benefit of the Tesla offer. In Southern California, one of the most popular routes was the trip from Los Angeles to Las Vegas. His estimations showed that this would be a profitable route, especially because people usually travel to Vegas in groups. The $100 ticket price per passenger from Los Angeles to Vegas would be similar to what bus-operated shuttle companies offered, but would be much cheaper than it would cost to take the trip in a car with a popular rideshare service.

While establishing his business strategy, it was extremely important to identify realistic risks and problems that had the potential to significantly alter or jeopardize business success. Would a car accident put his car out of business for months due to the lack of available replacement parts? Would a change in the free fuel policy destroy his business? You can never eliminate all risk from a business venture, but you can try to minimize risk to the best of your ability. Haydn prepared a list of more than 200 questions and visited his nearest Tesla dealership to speak with representatives that could help iron out more of his logistic questions. Fortunately, the staff at the store were very supportive of his plans and provided him with the answers he needed, in addition to a few extra considerations and possibilities. During this process, Haydn was also reassured that the "free charging for life" policy would be permanently extended to all owners that purchased the car during the promotion window. However, Haydn had started thinking ahead, and he figured that his future business could still thrive with an anticipated fuel expense of $.06 per mile. The free charging promotion was great for launching the business, but a sustainable business model would be sure to secure profit margins even after paying for fuel.

In the summer of 2015, Haydn leased the car and officially launched his microbusiness. With the idea of providing roundtrip shuttle service in a Tesla, he decided to name the business "Tesloop." He had given himself three months to prove that he could sustainably earn more than the cost of the car, and if he couldn't then he'd be able to return the car to Tesla as stated in the Happiness Guarantee. Haydn immediately locked into the focus of creating a unique customer experience, with an internal mission of making a ride in the Tesla feel like a "Starbucks on wheels." Not only did he provide snacks and beverages, but he also made sure that customers were able to charge their phones and laptops during the commute.

To promote his microbusiness, Haydn designed targeted social media ads, and was able to make adjustments based on the analytics he received to let him know how his posts were performing. Haydn was able to release ads to specific cities and age groups, but in the very beginning word-of-mouth advertising proved to be the most effective. Haydn and the people he knew would even talk to people during long-distance train rides and inform them of the alternative travel arrangement that his new Tesloop service provided.

It didn't take long for Tesloop demand to take off. His car was completing its routes with sold-out seating, and the need for a second car became clear if Haydn wanted Tesloop to continue to grow and serve new customers. Haydn decided for himself that he should scale the business and add more cars to his fleet, and from the moment he bought his second car, his microbusiness phase was complete. He had gathered enough validation to decide that he wanted to invest the additional time and money necessary to dedicate full-time hours to the business. The microbusiness had complemented his lifestyle and enabled him to own and drive a car that would otherwise be out of reach. As a result, the car basically paid for itself, but Haydn saw opportunity and wanted to see how successful his business could be if he had leased additional Tesla vehicles to expand his shuttle service.

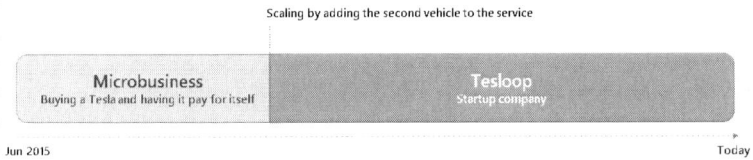

By 2018, Tesloop had over 120 employees and an expanded fleet in which each car was bringing in over $17,000 in revenue each month. The customer service was amazing, and the shuttle provided a premium experience that made Tesloop the preferred method of travel for many people heading to Vegas, Palm Springs, or San Diego from Los Angeles or Orange County. Tesloop even developed their own routing software to optimize rides and make sure that the shuttles were arriving on-time, after picking up passengers along the way. The service had expanded significantly, and had come a long way from being just an idea from a teenager wanting to drive an amazing car.

As the year went on, a series of unfortunate events had taken place, which included regulatory changes regarding passenger reservation capabilities and driver costs. The customer experience was negatively affected by policies stating that passengers could no longer reserve rear seats in the vehicle. The new policies had caused a shift in his employment structure that led to a 30 percent increase in driver cost, making it extremely difficult to earn profit from operating the company. Haydn had tried to find creative solutions to the new problems, but in October of 2018, he made the decision to suspend the service.

Today, Haydn is resuming Tesloop with a restructured product offering that essentially enables long distance car rentals between cities. As a kid who had been captivated by the launch of the very first Tesla vehicle, Haydn has pivoted his attention from one Tesla-based business model to the next. With his genuine interest in the vehicles, his vast knowledge of Tesla, and his understanding of Tesla's customer base, Haydn has the necessary insight to solve problems for others and identify business opportunities. Overall, we're excited to see where Haydn's path leads, and we wish him the best.

Tesloop began as a microbusiness and evolved into Haydn's first formal business venture, but during our interview with him, we found that he did have prior microbusiness experience. A little-known fact about Haydn is that he really enjoyed gaming when he was around thirteen-years-old, and he'd been managing a group of gamers, also known as a "clan," in his free time. These clans would compete together against other gamers, and some of the most successful clans were able to monetize heavily by winning tournaments and receiving YouTube advertisement revenue from their gameplay videos. Haydn was the leader of his clan, and engaged in a range of activities from marketing to recruiting to organizing member roles. His clan amassed several thousand followers, and he says that it was "like running a business."

This experience provided him his first true leadership experience, and in addition to the collaboration and management skills he learned, this was the first time in which he encountered the seemingly infinite potential return on time invested in a business activity. Haydn saw that there was a direct correlation with his clan's success and the amount of time he put into it, and he learned that operating a business could have limitless potential. In school, teachers normally provide an explanation of how a student can earn an "A" in the class, but through the development of his clan-based microbusiness, Haydn learned that he could generate his own approach and utilize every available resource to build something new. It was a different learning experience, but one that definitely influenced his ability to lead Tesloop to become the highest-rated transportation application of all time.

As we conclude this chapter, we'd like to pass on a few messages from Haydn. He was only age sixteen when he began Tesloop, but with the experience that he's gathered from building such a large company, Haydn outlined eleven key tips to help his fellow entrepreneurial teens and young people succeed:

1) Always ask questions. Try to get as deep of an understanding about subjects as you can.

2) Speak with as many people as you can about your idea. Try to understand where the doubts are coming from, and figure out how to address the main concerns.

3) Gather as many relevant metrics as you can and try to base decisions upon them. If you are undecided on a direction you want to go, step out of your shoes and ask yourself what guidance you would give somebody else facing the same position. If that differs from what you are doing, ask yourself why.

4) Be humble and never complacent. There are always ways to improve.

5) There are many ways to solve every problem. Determining the best approach is the challenge. There are no answers in the back of the book. Critical thinking is very important.

6) Surround yourself with A+ people. Depending on your environment, your friends may not be the right people.

7) Start small but always have a growth vision and plan of action for next steps.

8) Try to understand and leverage your strengths/weaknesses. Find the balance between staying focused and being a polymath. Don't get lost in unimportant details.

9) Get good at public speaking and work on interpersonal skills. Very important to convey confidence to those around you.

10) Don't get caught up in setbacks. Use learnings from the past to inform future decisions.

11) Finally, think of everything as a learning experience. If you succeed (monetarily, socially, etc.) that's a bonus, but not the goal.

Case Study #2: Building BLOC / Oppti

"I think that's the single best piece of advice: constantly think about how you could be doing things better and questioning yourself."

-Elon Musk

Building BLOC is a non-profit company that helps high school students with college and career development. Oppti is a software company that helps high school students identify potential opportunities to engage with employers via internship, volunteering, and various events. After the first six months of operation, the partnership between Building BLOC and Oppti went on to impact fifty-nine high schools, with more than 106,000 students. Both companies were birthed from the same microbusiness, and the software became one of the fastest growing educational technology solutions in the country. How did Building BLOC and Oppti achieve such quick success? The answer lies in the details.

After graduation, Weston and I were able to secure consulting jobs with KPMG and Deloitte, respectively. Only a few months had passed before we individually started thinking of ways to apply our skills to help people outside of our co-worker and client networks.

In September of 2017, Weston had been leading client engagements at KPMG, and was well on his way to his first promotion. At the same time, he was also looking into potential roles with the local municipality in hopes of helping his broader community. He learned about the impactful city roles that would help address critical issues, while allowing him to maintain his consulting job. The role that best suited him was the role of City Planning Commissioner, in which he could participate in bi-weekly meetings with four other Commissioners to vote on land use and development proposals throughout the city. However, after appropriately filing intent with KPMG, reaching out to staff in Washington D.C and even the CFO of the organization, it turned out that Weston was denied the possibility of being City Planning Commissioner while working at KPMG due to conflicts of interest. The major issue preventing Weston from pursuing the city role was the fact that technically he'd be able to vote and make decisions that would impact KPMG clients and employees. He was given an ultimatum: Choose between KPMG and helping the city in a formal capacity.

As the year 2017 came to a close, I remember reflecting about the deeply fulfilling consulting projects that I'd been working on, and how amazing it had been to have a critical role in developing strategies with C-level executives to improve company operations. I also remember thinking about my rough childhood and being grateful for the inspirational role models and mentors who I've met along the way that helped me persevere through hardship and adversity. For the New Year, I had the urge to pay forward the value of the guidance and support that I'd received by creating a blog in which I'd create and post motivational articles. With the trending popularity of "Life Hacks," the modern term to describe convenient tips posted by the Internet community to help increase productivity or efficiency, I decided that my page would be called "Motivation Hacks."

On December 29th, I created the Facebook page. To maximize effectiveness, I decided it was best to establish a few guiding principles for the articles I wanted to write. The articles had to be:

- Inspirational
- Short in length, approximately one-and-a-half pages
- Easy to read, but the feel should be perceived as casual/academic
- Connected to a popular figure via quotes or related actions and habits
- Personal, and able to communicate why the article was relevant to me

The articles were well-received on Facebook, and early readers commented on my posts with support and words of encouragement. I posted articles every week until my consulting work bled into my weekends enough to overwhelm my writing efforts. However, the process of posting these inspirational articles confirmed that I found enjoyment in sharing helpful content, and positively impacting those that found value in my thoughts.

Here's where the stars began to align. Weston's fight for KPMG to approve his pursuit of the City Planning Commissioner role lasted about seven months, and he was formally denied in March of 2018. During the same month, I authored and posted my last article for Motivation Hacks.

Weston and I put our heads together to find the right cause and methodology to maximize the positive impact we could bring to society. After a few discussions, we started to reflect on our pasts and our individual journeys. We realized that when we entered college, we didn't have a strong understanding of potential business careers. Through various on-campus experiences and summer internships, we were able to engage in work ranging from financial services to marketing. By pursuing and securing internships, we were able to learn what we liked and disliked, and it was very different from what high school prepared us for. What if we could help high school students develop a solid understanding of careers in business before entering college?

With this in mind we performed research to better understand the high school demographic to see how we could best help students interested in pursuing a career in business. We needed to answer questions such as:

- Is there a gap between how prepared students are and how prepared they would like to be for pursuing a career in business? How big is the problem?
- What would high school students want to learn about business?
- What would we offer?
- How many high schools should we initially work with?
- What should the name of our organization be?

Weston and I knew that there was a major difference between what we had known about business in high school and what we had learned by the time we were signing employment offers and preparing for graduation photos. It's easy to say that we wish we knew more about business when we were younger, but we had to validate whether current high school students had the desire to pursue knowledge in addition to what they were learning in school. Did the students want to find additional tutorials outside of the classroom? Or were the business lessons they learned in school more than enough to meet their needs? We had a strong hunch that there were kids from schools with limited resources who would love to have additional business guidance.

To figure out what high school students wanted to learn about business, Weston and I first contacted a few siblings of our friends, and we asked them to explain their current understanding of what it means to have a career in the field of business. One student said, "Business is when you own a company, people work for you, and your company sells stuff to people," while another student said, "Having a career in business means that you work long hours, you're greedy, and you're always selling things for more than they cost." We found that students are heavily influenced by the professions held by their family members and the stereotypes seen in movies. We would always probe a bit more and ask questions like, "Can a doctor be a businessperson? After a few of questions to gauge their understanding, we would elaborate more on the broader definition of business, and see if they would be interested in learning more about a specific area. Overall, we found that students asked about accounting and entrepreneurship, but they were also very happy to learn that business is present in every profession and industry. Even though students had different levels of business acumen, it seemed pretty clear that most students would greatly benefit from learning the fundamentals, and by having additional perspectives provided by professionals who could further elaborate on the business aspects of their jobs.

Weston and I saw that there were high school students who we could help develop a stronger understanding of business, and we decided to create a nonprofit dedicated to that cause. We wanted students to learn business fundamentals. After a couple days of thought, we decided to name the company "Building BLOC," with "BLOC" being an acronym for "Business Leaders of Orange County" in part due to our location, which quickly became "Business Leaders of California" to allow for growth throughout the state with the anticipation of a larger expansion. We checked online for availability and registered the company in the state of California.

After answering the above questions, we decided to reach out to a local high school in Westminster, California to see if we can start a career development club in which students can receive mentorship from recent college grads, while being able to learn more about careers in business. We figured that we would start with a small group of students that would apply to receive mentors. After a few referrals, we connected with a business teacher who told us that our timing was great and that he really believed that our Building BLOC efforts would be complementary to what he had been teaching them in class. He agreed that the students could largely benefit from mentorship and additional guidance, especially from people that were relatable and working professional jobs as recent college graduates. We collectively decided that a presentation to the student class would be best to launch our pilot program and establish our first group of mentees.

To prepare for our meeting with the class, Weston and I had to formalize our messaging and created a website and presentation deck in which we stated that our mission was to help students with varying levels of business interests and experiences to better understand personal and professional goals through peer-to-peer networking opportunities and hands-on experiences. It was also very important to us to let the students know that our plan was to work with the local community and foster close-knit and supportive networks for career development, leadership, and service. After a few working sessions, we determined that the key components of the summer pilot program would be to provide one-on-one mentorship to each of the participants, in addition to having them work collaboratively on a business project as well as a group volunteering event.

Weston and I decided that the students would have to apply to the pilot program. Not only would this allow us to gauge true interest in our program, but it would also enable us to distribute our mentor base with better efficiency. By asking students to answer a few questions, we could pair them with the mentor who would best meet their development needs. We reached out to a few people in our personal networks who we knew would make great mentors. We thought about their career success, the industries they were working in, their previous mentor/mentee experiences, and their overall communication styles. We secured our mentor base and started to prepare questions for the student application. The application would require students to answer questions about their expectations of the pilot program, and describe their academic and non-academic passions.

By the time the class presentation date arrived on our calendars, we were more than ready to make a solid first impression with the students, and we were excited to share all the benefits that we could bring to them on behalf of Building BLOC. We delivered an amazing presentation, and some of the students even submitted their application on the same day. After the review process, we accepted four students, and officially launched the program. We were able to pair them with mentors who were currently working in the exact fields that the students expressed interest in. It was amazing. Everyone was happy. The students received great mentors, and the mentors felt great sharing their knowledge with ambitious high school students. Our vision was materializing and we were positively impacting the community, just as we intended.

As the individual mentorships of the pilot program continued to develop, Weston and I were sure to stay in constant communication with both the mentor and mentee groups. We wanted the one-on-one mentorships to be custom experiences for each of the students, meaning that if one student wanted to discuss resumes during their first session, and another student wanted to discuss the college application process during their first session, then both students could receive the information that they were most curious about, without needing to coordinate with the rest of the program. However, the Building BLOC mentor and mentee groups did get together to clean up a local beach, and the students even enjoyed the experience of gaining new perspectives from discussions with the mentors of other students.

We concluded the pilot program with a group business project in which the students would study an actual business case from the Harvard Business School. The assignment was for the students to learn about Netflix, with a specific focus on the business decisions that the company made and how they were able to beat their early competitors to become the most dominant streaming platform for movies and videos. The students would then write a report on the company to confirm understanding and communicate insight gathered from the description of how Netflix positioned itself for success. Lastly, they also put together a presentation deck in which they neatly packaged their key points, and even communicated what they would do if they were leading Netflix today.

At the end of the pilot program, all four of the students elected to continue with the program and take-on leadership roles within the Building BLOC School Club. They were passionate about recruiting additional students, and were able to grow from four members to thirty members in just a few months. Of the thirty members, we expanded our mentor-mentee offering to a total of ten students. While helping the students with college and career activities, we realized that there was a broader problem that students and mentors were communicating to us. What we found was that many students had difficulty finding opportunities to intern or volunteer. They would search on Google, or use many of the "job-finder" services on the Web, but searching for opportunities usually led to the discovery of countless opportunities that didn't quite satisfy what they were looking for. For example, if a student searched for "high school internships," the results would contain many internships for college students to intern at a high school or school district, in addition to internships that had listed "high school diploma required" in their criteria to determine candidate eligibility.

To address this problem, some of the mentors began searching online to help their mentees find opportunities, and we were able to aggregate some of the postings from nearby organizations into a spreadsheet. We would then refer to this spreadsheet whenever a mentee was ready to discuss ways in which they could further enrich their resumes and gain experience in the fields that interested them. However, it became clear that we had evolved into being the custodians of this opportunity list, and it had dawned on us that there could be millions of high school students out there that would benefit from having a directory to help them find internships and volunteering experiences. Weston and I knew that it was time to look into building a website where high school students could access an opportunity directory, at any time of the day, and from any city in the United States.

We identified a problem that high school students were experiencing, and our spreadsheet of opportunities had seemed to be a quick, temporary fix. To increase the robustness of our solution, we thought that it would be extremely valuable to create a website that would allow us to upload high school-aged internships and volunteering experiences that we found online, and we would continue to aggregate opportunities for the students. Weston and I decided to move forward with our microbusiness idea to create a platform where students could find opportunities, employers could post opportunities, and school counselors could help facilitate the arrangement where necessary. In alignment with our definition of what constitutes a microbusiness, we were looking to create a microbusiness because we wanted to form an organization consisting of one or two people who initiate exchanges that served a social cause. Originally, we didn't have a strong understanding of how much anyone would be willing to pay for our website, but we offered it for free and focused on the value that we could deliver to the students and the community. Considering that California is often considered to be a leader in educational development and values, it was reasonable to assume that if students in California could benefit from the solution, so could many students around the country.

We were based in Southern California, but we were well aware of the ways in which our Silicon Valley neighbors in the Northern part of the state had developed prominent philosophies for creating startup companies. "The Lean Startup," by Eric Ries, was widely praised for emphasizing the concept of releasing a product while actively soliciting feedback to further validate for confirmation and make necessary revisions along the way. Ries explains that this iterative process helps reduce costs, and prevents entrepreneurs from making the mistake of investing time and money into a product that nobody wanted to buy or use. Reid Hoffman, founder of LinkedIn, is responsible for a well-known quote that has reverberated throughout the startup community: "If you're not embarrassed by the first version of your product, you've launched too late."

Knowing that we wanted to launch a website, we began to review website builders to find the best one for us to create a beautified version of our spreadsheet containing internship and volunteer opportunities for students. Weston didn't have a coding background, and neither did I, so we chose to use the Wix platform because it offered an easy-to-use interface, but also accepted lines of code to make modifications as we became more proficient or brought in additional resources over time. Before creating the website, we had to plan the exact features we wanted to launch for the initial rollout. We had to list the key stakeholders and map out their experiences. In those early weeks, the best name that we had at the time was "Job Lobby," so we went with it.

The name "Job Lobby" was chosen because the physical lobby of a company's office location is where students usually develop their first real impression of the company's look and feel. In the lobby is where many students form stronger perceptions of company culture and employee personalities, which leads the student to envision their lives as a future new-hire. We went with "Job Lobby" and continued to build out the website. There was an early understanding that we would change the name if something better came along, but there was a lot that we could create within Wix before securing the domain or registering the company. We were still employed at our consulting jobs during the day, we worked nights and weekends to bring this solution to life.

Job Lobby. With an emphasis on jobs, rather than the internship and volunteer experiences, we felt that the name didn't quite represent the full set of opportunities that students pursued in high school. After a short period, we learned that we'd eventually want to include events, apprenticeships, and opportunities for job shadowing, and we couldn't quite find a name that captured all the potential listings that students could apply for. In conversation with each other, we started to refer to the potential listings as "opportunities," simply because it was much more convenient than mentioning all the specific post types that employers could provide for students. One day it dawned on us: Why don't we just use a name that represented all the different types of opportunities that students could apply for? We shortened "opportunity" and tried "Oppti." As soon as we said it, we said it again, and again, and knew that it felt right. Weston and I immediately looked online to see if there were any established companies with that name, and also checked for different variations of "Oppti." After testing out "Optee," "Oppty," and everything else you could imagine, we made it official, and Oppti was born.

Weston and I had a solid enough understanding of the problem and our proposed solution to move forward with building out our first version of Oppti, but we still had to perform research to find answers to important questions like the ones below:

- Were there any websites or mobile apps that aggregated opportunities exclusively for high school students? If not, were there any sites that gave users the ability to filter for opportunities for students who were fourteen to eighteen years old?
- Were high school counselors and staff referring students to any particular Internet-based resource? How were the career center specialists and counselors helping students find opportunities?
- Did other schools have the same problem? Is there a difference between how well-funded high schools help students find opportunities and the way that high schools with tight budgets try to address the issue?
- From the schools and districts, were there any current practices around screening opportunities for students to protect their safety and make sure they were applying to legitimate organizations?

When Weston and I searched online to find companies that were trying to address the same problem, we found countless websites that were established to help college students find resources, but nothing for high school students. It seemed like opportunities were hard to find for students that were still enrolled in high school, and that the opportunities were primarily targeting recent high school grads, or those that turned eighteen-years-old before the end of their senior year. The question, "What opportunities to build career experience do I have as a sixteen-year-old?" largely went unanswered.

Looking a bit further, we found that certain Fortune 500 companies would post summer internships for high school students, but that the advertisement of those opportunities had room for improvement. For example, a company like Microsoft may have posted a summer internship position for active high school students, but for many students, the only way that they would find out about that opportunity is if they happened to directly visit the Microsoft webpage to browse internship posts. We immediately thought about the many high school students that would've been genuinely interested in applying, if only they knew that such an opportunity existed. Weston and I also had to check to see if there were websites that listed opportunities for all ages, that maybe contained the functionality to filter opportunities based on ages fourteen to eighteen and included an age filter for students. At best, we were able to find sites that were dedicated directories for teens to find local volunteer opportunities, but those sites would still leave students to look elsewhere for available internships, job shadowing, and other beneficial engagements with employers.

To further our search, we wanted to find out more about what high school counselors were doing to address this problem. After a series of phone calls and emails, we found that school counselors performed many functions, from helping high school students apply for college or find scholarships, to helping students with much needed career advice. We also found that some schools had higher counselor-to-student ratios, meaning that they were able to either spend more time per student, or engage in more activities that would benefit the entire student body. There were a handful of schools in which the counselor had put together a newsletter or spreadsheet containing opportunities, but this had proved to be a rare finding. We learned that employers send flyers or emails to school counselors, and schools have different processes around how they review the opportunities and share them with students. Some schools would leave copies of the flyers in the office for students to view while waiting for their appointments, and we also encountered a software solution that allowed counselors to upload flyers for students to browse. These were the solutions that were being implemented, but they lack the type of robustness that would result from having a dedicated software system for student employment opportunities.

From school counselors to district directors, there were many different approaches to address the difficulty that high school students had in finding opportunities, and we received further validation that it would be extremely beneficial for students, companies, and schools to have a centralized database that could host an aggregated list of opportunities for students aged fourteen to eighteen. We thought that schools enforcing a graduation requirement of a specified number of service hours would have better processes in place to help students find opportunities, but this was not necessarily the case. Many schools wanted to help students find employment experiences, but the problem seemed too big to solve when considering the additional duties of school counselors. It turned out that schools with more resources generally did a better job of closing the opportunity gap for students. This was an interesting find, and it deepened our resolve to build out the software and share opportunities with students who received less information about internships and volunteering just because they didn't have a true view of what was available to them.

Regarding the approach of how schools and districts chose to screen opportunities for the students, it became clear that there was no standardized approach. Some schools performed low levels of screening, but specified that the parents/guardians were solely responsible for thoroughly reviewing opportunities, while some schools sent incoming opportunities to the district for approval. Weston and I shared an understanding that the safety of the high school students was to be kept in high priority, and that we would have to work with more education professionals to further understand how our solution would comply with the various screening methods for student engagement with employers.

When we started, we had performed research and gathered enough information from the Building BLOC students to develop a certain level of confidence, but we continued to learn more about the schools, students, and employers as we moved forward. Connecting with schools around the country, we would gather new insights from schools on the East Coast that contributed to the overall collection of data regarding best practices to implement.

In January of 2019, we officially launched Oppti as an MVP, meaning "Minimum Viable Product" as popularized from "The Lean Startup." An MVP is a product that has only the most necessary features, and it enables a company to begin gathering feedback from customers who adopt early. Guy Kawasaki, in his book "The Art of the Start 2.0," furthers this concept by writing that companies should develop an "MVVVP." Kawasaki adds the additional letters to make the distinction that not only should the initial launch be viable, but it should also be "valuable" and "validating." With this rationale, the launch of a product or service should be treated as an efficient experiment in which the market confirms or rejects your hypothesis, and communicates how much demand exists for what you've created. This "MVVVP" is exactly what the initial version of Oppti was.

If you browse the Oppti website today, you wouldn't believe that it started out with a plain white background and a minimalistic, basic design. Every company has to start somewhere, and as a microbusiness, this version of Oppti was good enough to start validating that our solution could scale and be valuable to many users.

The student user journey for Oppti was constructed as follows:

1) Schools would share our website with their high school students via email or by posting our site on the school page.
2) Students would access our homepage.
3) Students created a profile and submitted basic information about themselves.
4) Students confirmed their profile information and proceeded to the available opportunities page to browse opportunities.
5) Students clicked "apply" on an opportunity that interests them, and a new tab opens on their browser that directs them to the employer's application page.

As you can see, the early Oppti website only had a few student-focused pages, and since we populated the original opportunities based on what we found in the area, you could even say that our site started as more of a directory rather than a platform. However, once we had a significant amount of student users, employers were happy to share opportunities directly to our website, which created a healthy platform that fueled further growth. When more attractive employers presented opportunities on the platform, it became more attractive to the students, and the overall platform became enriched by the mutual enthusiasm of various user groups.

At first, Weston and I wanted to provide a platform where students could apply for internships and volunteering opportunities within our site, and we had a lot of features planned, but we had to minimize the features that were present in the first version. The effort required to build out a robust system where everything happens within Oppti was beyond feasibility due to technical and time-based constraints. We wanted to launch a version of Oppti that would maximize impact for students, and when focusing on the core functionality of what we wanted to offer, it was clear that we could direct students to the URL links of the employer application pages, rather than delaying our launch due to technical difficulty. Even though we wouldn't necessarily be able to measure how many students were successfully securing opportunities, we were still able to help the students discover them, and we figured that this simplified value proposition was still helpful to school staff.

Weston and I received good feedback from the first high school we worked with, and overall, we felt that we received the validation necessary for our microbusiness to graduate into a legitimate startup. We felt that our days of helping high school students find internships and volunteer opportunities were only beginning. The problem that we were solving was huge, and the available solutions were essentially non-existent, but if we wanted to maximize our ability to grow, then we would have to best position Oppti to thrive.

Considering the fact that it would be very expensive to hire developers and properly serve such a large population of students, schools, and employers, we felt that a non-profit structure would limit our ability to raise funds. Building BLOC had been receiving money from donations and fundraisers, while providing services to schools at no charge. To develop Oppti and share it with as many students as possible, we thought it would be beneficial for us to have the ability to receive investment from Venture Capital funds or parties interested in receiving a small piece of the company in exchange for funding rapid growth. Non-profit companies don't have that option, so we decided to establish Oppti as a separate entity. Typically, software companies easily spend over $100,000 on initial development, and Oppti as a for-profit company could raise the funds necessary to support that kind of capital-intensive infrastructure. This approach would enable us to continue to provide schools with free and low-cost options for helping high school students find internship and volunteer opportunities. Soon after registering Oppti as an official company, we left our consulting jobs and dedicated ourselves to full-time development. We increased the pace at which we began onboarding schools, and the rest was history.

Looking at the overall success story of Building BLOC and Oppti, it all began with two good friends who were looking to positively impact their community. Our initial efforts led to the establishment of a microbusiness providing college and career development help to high school students. This microbusiness allowed us to validate a business idea, while solving problems for students in our community. This microbusiness turned into a non-profit company. It also provided us with new information and inspired us to pursue the development of a second microbusiness, one that was created to test the validity of designing a software solution that could help students find internships and volunteer opportunities. The second microbusiness developed into Oppti, a startup company, and we continued to grow in alignment with Building BLOC.

By working in parallel, Oppti helped Building BLOC make the transition from a local to a national non-profit company because we were able to promote college and career development clubs at schools that were initially excited about implementing just the software. The companies were complementary to each other. We had a dual mission of expanding the number schools with Building BLOC club-members, and growing Oppti's user participation in helping high school students secure internships and volunteer opportunities.

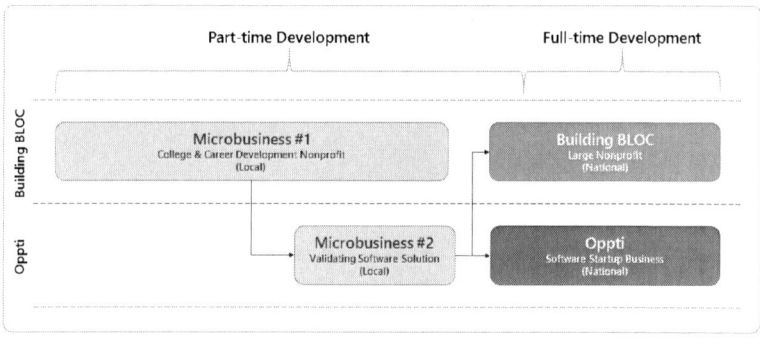

Building BLOC and Oppti both have great social impact today, serving over hundred high schools, but the two organizations would not have succeeded without the rigorous planning and the necessary adaptability that we had to embrace upon receiving new, valuable information. We put a lot of thought into each plan that we created, and as we executed each critical step, Weston and I made sure to fully absorb the resulting new information so that we could have the chance to revise and improve our approach.

Today, the most fulfilling part of our work is the feedback that we receive from students, school staff, and employers. Building BLOC students have used their experiences to gain admission into some of the finest universities, and they've also communicated that they've been able to find more opportunities than ever before. We've had school districts tell us that our solution is exactly what they've been trying to develop, and that it aligns deeply with initiatives to increase student internships by 10 percent and to help students complete their graduation-based, service-learning required hours. Employers communicated that our website was launched just as they began focusing additional recruitment efforts on high school students, and that our solution saved them time and helped them provide fulfilling experiences to more students.

One of the major takeaways here is that you can start a social impact-driven microbusiness, and develop a strong business by being passionate about helping others. It's also important to note that the local version of Building BLOC was successful and sustainable on its own as a microbusiness, and did not need to grow to a national level just to be considered successful. If you want to maintain your micro-business without scaling to a larger operation, that's totally okay, as long as it satisfies your personal goals. Now that you've read the case studies that we've described, you can proceed to the next chapter to learn how you can approach starting your own microbusiness.

PART III:
ROADMAP FOR LAUNCHING
YOUR MICROBUSINESS

10-STEP ROADMAP: OVERVIEW

"Without strategy, execution is aimless. Without
execution, strategy is useless."

-Morris Cheng

Of the most popular questions we hear from aspiring entrepreneurs, the first is usually some variation of, "I want to get started
and pursue a business idea, but where do I start?" With all the mis-
conceptions out there, it is important for you to understand that there
are many business ideas that can be developed without expensive
investments, massive amounts of time, or a "genius" team of founders. Today, depending on the type of idea, you may be able to start with
a few dollars and a free social media account. For example, if you
handcraft a product based on a $10 purchase of raw materials, and
use social media to post and promote your work, which then sells for
$15-30, you may have a sustainable microbusiness that can teach you
a lot about order fulfillment, demand management, and more.

You've read our case studies, and you've seen very specific
examples of how an idea can become a microbusiness, and now you

want to know how you can get started on your own. To help with this, Weston and I created a roadmap with a step-by-step breakdown of how you can create your own microbusiness. Of course, there are other ways to get started, but we created this method because it enables you to plan ahead and take calculated steps to improve your success rate. There are some people that stumble into a business idea, but we wouldn't be helping if we were advising you to wait until you get lucky. This method will break down the microbusiness process into ten simple steps that will allow you to identify, initiate, and execute business ideas. Before you initiate your business idea, we believe that there are six things you should do that can better prepare you for the outcome you're looking to have.

Microbusiness Roadmap

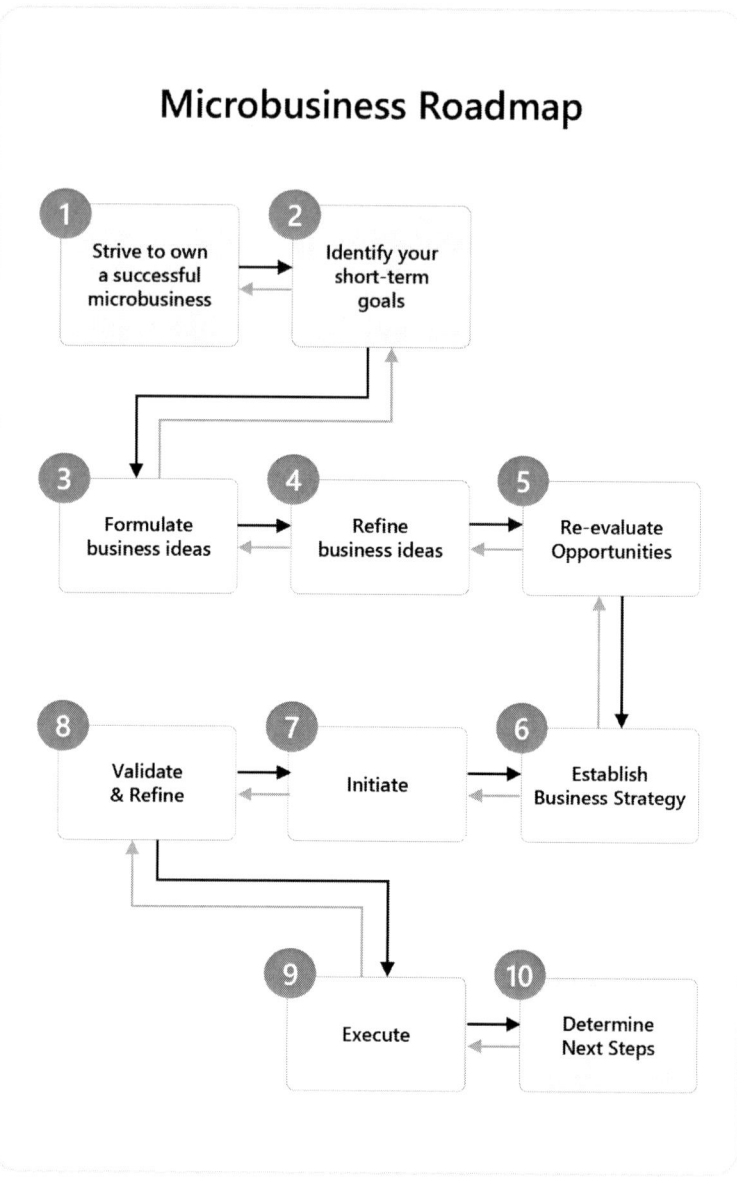

Step 1 – Striving to Own a Successful Microbusiness

As you've already made the decision to read this book, it's safe to assume that operating a successful microbusiness is something you can see yourself doing. If this is indeed the case, then you are well on your way to completing the first step. You must strive to own a successful microbusiness. In life, there are lots of jobs that you can apply to, but it feels fantastic to have a job that you have created for yourself and truly enjoy. From wanting to be the founder of a billion-dollar tech company, to wanting to create a large plastic recycling company, experimentation with smaller scale operations will help prepare you for the higher levels of entrepreneurship. You'll learn how to manage your resources to persevere and achieve a desired outcome. Today, you may have $100 to spend on raw materials, shipping, and marketing, and the lessons you learn from this experience will help you in the future, even if you have hundreds of thousands of dollars or more to support your business operations later on.

In the introduction of this book, we mentioned a few reasons why others choose a path of entrepreneurship, but it's important for you to have your own "why." You need to understand why you want to become a microbusiness owner. From our experience, the "why" is what keeps you engaged when you encounter difficulties. Today, entrepreneurship is more accessible than ever, and it is often romanticized, but if you don't know why you're doing it, you may have a hard time. There are some important questions that you must ask yourself when you are deciding whether you want to pursue the creation of a microbusiness. Do you enjoy making leadership decisions? Some people like to operate under the establishment of clear directions, and may even get anxious when making heavy decisions.

When starting your own microbusiness, know that it's different from your experience in school. Just as Haydn said earlier, in school you receive a guideline in which if you do everything well, you can earn an "A." However, in business, and even in a microbusiness, you are the one setting the guidelines for yourself.

In anticipation of the entrepreneurial journey, know that this is not the most common path for people to take. Know that if it was easy, there would be a lot more entrepreneurs than there are now. Know that others may discourage you from starting by saying that you should just stick to whatever you're currently doing, or they may advise you that it's better to do what most of the other people are doing at your age. There's nothing wrong with achieving great academic success, looking for internships, or trying to find the right job, but entrepreneurship offers a chance to create an invaluable business experience for yourself.

For many people, the thought of creating a business is scary. The fear of failure. The difficulty. The risk. Thankfully, creating a microbusiness will help to ease these concerns. Compared to a business that requires you to spend a lot of money upfront, a microbusiness decreases the risk by reducing the amount of capital necessary to begin operating, therefore reducing the loss amount if the business is discontinued. Also, because microbusinesses start small, the level of difficulty is much more manageable than the hardship encountered when managing several employees or a multitude of product lines.

When trying to determine if launching a microbusiness is right for you, it's important to address the fear of failure. To do this, you must think about how the microbusiness could reasonably play out, and understand the pros and cons. Here's a scenario: You want to launch a cookie company, so you start by making cookies with your friends and selling them in your neighborhood to first see if people like your cookies. You spend $11 on cookie ingredients, and you happen to already have some baking materials in your kitchen. You make fifty-one cookies with the intension of selling them for $1 each or $2 for three. In the best outcome you earn $51 in revenue, which equates to a $40 profit. If you still sell all your cookies, but everyone buys them three at a time, then you earn $34 in revenue, and a $23 profit. We've established that if you sell all your cookies, you will earn between $23 and $40 in profit.

Revenue – (# sold x price/cookie)	$0 to $51
Cost – (Cookie ingredients)	-$11
Profit Range	-$11 to $40

Now, let's think about how many cookies you would have to sell to at least earn back the $11 that you put into it. You would either must sell eleven cookies individually, or six bundles of three cookies. If you're able to sell at least the amount for you to break even, then you've only lost the time and energy you put into ending up with the same amount of money you started with. However, throughout that process, you've gained relevant knowledge in the following business aspects: Procurement and supply chain management, and financial forecasting.

Potential Breakeven points	$1 (for each cookie)	$2 (for 3 cookies)	Total Revenue
Breakeven #1	11 cookies	0 bundles	$11
Breakeven #2	0 cookies	6 bundles (18 cookies)	$12
Breakeven #3	5 cookies	3 bundles (9 cookies)	$11

If you reflected on your sales performance, you could even hypothesize about steps you could take to refine your approach if you choose to try again. Would you try another cookie type, or another neighborhood? Did your customers say things like, "If you had 'x', then I would buy 'y' number of cookies, or pay 'z' amount of dollars," while you were engaging with them? If yes, then even if you didn't profit from your initial cookie sales, you have gained invaluable experience that can directly be applied to future business ideas or a second attempt at the same business.

For measuring success with your microbusiness, it is important to look beyond financial results. Even if you only sold one cookie, you would have fifty cookies remaining, at a cost of $.20 per cookie that you can enjoy for yourself. With everything that you most likely learned throughout this attempt, we would say that it is well worth the $10 that you had to pay. In the worst-case scenario, you sell no cookies and you lose $11 and a couple hours of effort in exchange for some valuable business lessons. Is the possibility of realizing this outcome enough to discourage you from trying?

Don't you find it interesting that what may have initially been a fear of failure could be also perceived as a fear of losing $11, and a little bit of time and effort. If you view it as a business experiment, truly embrace the lessons learned. Try to make revisions to the same idea or pivot to something else, but know that your failure only moves you one step closer to success. As Arianna Huffington said, "Failure is not the opposite of success. It is the stepping stone to success."

With a solid grasp on the downside of starting a microbusiness, you should be encouraged to create one. If you suspect that your life will be better as a business owner, follow that hunch, and start small with a microbusiness. If you succeed, you win, and if you fail, you still win because your lessons are greater than your losses. Strive to own a successful microbusiness.

Step 2 – Identifying Goals

What are you looking to achieve over the next few years? Whether you're trying to get into a good school for your next step in the academic realm, or looking to obtain basic business experience out of curiosity, it's extremely important for you to be aligned with your goals. By identifying your goals, you will solidify your understanding of what is driving your decisions. Are you trying to invent something that redefines how we exist in our everyday lives? Are you trying to establish passive income to better fund activities with friends? Remember, Tesloop's initial success can be attributed to Haydn's original effort to find a creative way to own his favorite car, even though it was too expensive for him to purchase at the time.

When you identify your goals, you are providing an important input into your microbusiness plan. Think of it like a GPS system. Every day, millions of people use GPS technology to get from their current location to their desired destination, and in many cases, the journey would prove extremely difficult to navigate without the automated assistance. One of the reasons that we love GPS so much is because once we type in where we're going, the technology finds the best routes for us to take by comparing possibilities and creating paths that minimize complications. Similarly, identifying your goals will help you determine if your microbusiness idea is capable of helping you reach those goals, because your microbusiness idea should be in alignment with your goals. For example, if you had a goal of wanting to become a make-up artist that helps customers find their inner-confidence, then you would always be able to check whether your microbusiness idea is helping you get closer to realizing that goal.

Your goals heavily influence both the microbusiness you decide to pursue and the strategy you deploy. Remember the GPS analogy. If your goals provide you with the destination, think of your microbusiness idea as the vehicle you can operate to complete the journey. There are many vehicles that you can take, but some may be more enjoyable or easier to operate than others.

As your microbusiness develops later on, you'll really appreciate the time you took to first understand your goals. We can't stress this enough: Your goals will heavily influence how you decide to grow. Identifying your goals beforehand is highly recommended because it will help you decide how experimental, conservative, or aggressive you want to be. For example, if you buy five products in a foreign market for $2 dollars, and successfully sell them in your local market for $4 dollars, then you may feel a certain amount of comfort around the sustainability of that business model. Drawing on that initial success, people will have different risk profiles and goals that will determine their next steps. For the second batch of products, those with aggressive goals may choose to invest a large amount of money to buy the same product because they feel they've received enough validation, while those with conservative goals may choose to buy a slightly larger quantity than they bought in the first batch, and experimental types may buy the same quantity of a similar product to compare results. Of course, you can experiment aggressively or conservatively, but everything ties back to the goals that you've set for yourself. By first determining your goals, you are able to establish guiding principles that help you decide how much risk you want to take on and how fast you need to move to achieve success.

In terms of learning how to actually establish goals for yourself, there is a popular framework that helps people set S.M.A.R.T goals, which stands for "specific, measurable, acceptable, realistic, and time-bound." The method is thoroughly described in Peter Drucker's book, **Management by Objectives**, in reference to organizations, but this framework applies well to personal goal-setting as well. If you used this framework to establish a personal goal, you might create a goal similar to the following: "I want to buy and sell sneakers online to earn enough money to pay for a ski-trip with my friends by the end of the year." This goal is specific because it firmly establishes what the activity is that will be performed (selling sneakers), and it specifies how it will be completed (online sales). This goal is also measurable because you can compute how much money you'd need to earn for the ski-trip, and constantly be aware of how many additional shoes you'd have to sell online to meet your goal. With today's technology, the goal is both acceptable and realistic, and it's time-bound because we know that you have until the end of the year to meet your target.

When setting these goals for yourself, it could also be helpful if you perform a self-assessment to better understand **your skills and interest areas.** This assessment will help you understand your capabilities, and might lead you to a business idea that can be relatively easy to begin. For example, if you have great marketing skills and online popularity, enjoy posting on social media, have access to people struggling to increase their website viewership, and want to pursue a business idea that has little cost and great flexibility around your busy schedule, you may be able to succeed with a microbusiness in which you advise on social media posts or post directly to your fan base to boost popularity for your clients.

The first part of the self-assessment is to understand your skills. Whether you're an amazing Math student, a brilliant violinist, or a high-performing athlete, writing down your five strongest skills will allow you to understand the capabilities that you can apply toward an area that interests you. You can even divide your skills into three categories: "Excellent," "Great," and "Good." Sometimes, a viable business idea may result from a "Good" skill of yours, paired with the excellent resources you have access to. You can also ask your family members or close friends to help you identify what your strengths are, but you'll want to avoid asking questions that steer them toward a particular answer. Questions like, "You think I'm a great communicator, right?" will contaminate the usability of your interpersonal survey. Hopefully, this process will serve at least one of two purposes: Affirm the skills that you've already identified, or remind you of additional skills that you possess.

The second part of the self-assessment is to understand your interest areas, and how they might align with your skills. The idea here is to tap into your feelings of curiosity, enjoyment, and fulfillment. Think about the topics you like to learn about and the pages you subscribe to online. You should also write down the things that you enjoy or derive pleasure from because we believe that there is some truth to the saying, "Choose a job you love, and you will never have to work a day in your life."

Your goals could be in alignment with your current skills, but this is not always the case. It's possible that you developed a skill in an area that you no longer find interesting, and you could also be interested in activities in which you currently possess no particular skill. If you were to create a Venn diagram out of your skills and interests, you would be able to see the center area where your interests and skills overlap. This center highlights the opportunities that may be the most useful inputs for establishing your goals. The interest-only portion will show areas in which you may need to further develop your skills to execute a sustainable microbusiness idea. The skills-only portion is good for your self-assessment and understanding, but it would be ill-advised to create goals in areas that you're not even interested in.

Ultimately, your goals will determine how much time, money, and effort you are willing to dedicate to building a microbusiness. Here are the two questions you can ask yourself to evaluate the ease or difficulty associated with meeting your goals. Are your goals aligned with:

1)   A strong skill of yours or something you have a lot of experience with?
2) A skill, area, or industry of great interest to you?

After setting S.M.A.R.T goals and completing your self-assessment, you should be ready to explore business ideas and find something that aligns well with the vision that you see for yourself in the future. Setting goals will help you understand what you're expecting to get out of the experience, and guide your allocation of resources, while helping you gauge the appropriate amount of risk. If your goal is to make as much money as you can, then your choices will be very different than someone who wants to allocate one or two hours per week to doing something fun that happens to bring in a few extra dollars.

Step 3 – Formulating Business Ideas

As stated in Step 2, if you rely on your goals to establish your microbusiness "GPS" destination, then your business idea will serve as the vehicle that you'll take to complete the journey. If your primary goal is to make an extra $200 per week, your path could be very different from the path of someone who has the primary goal of creating a new resource in the community. Of course, it is also possible to accomplish both goals in parallel, but your goals would have to clearly establish that you're trying to do both.

While reading the case studies that we've covered earlier in the book, you saw that businesses vary greatly in terms of the circumstances that led to creation. In this section, we will thoroughly describe two primary methods for you to develop seemingly viable ideas. The first method builds upon your self-assessment to find a microbusiness opportunity that can work for you, and the second method focuses on finding problems and coming up with creative solutions.

By revisiting the results from your self-assessment, you might discover many microbusiness ideas, and you can review your skills and interests to see what your unique opportunities may be. What we want to do is understand how your resources can support business ideas in areas where you have great skill and interest. Resources can include people, materials, money, or any asset that would allow you to progress your microbusiness. We consider a resource to be determined by two sets of criteria; is it direct or indirect, and how important of a role do you expect it to play in your success?

Determining whether a resource is direct or indirect is pretty straightforward. If you need a camera to launch a small photography business, do you already own one of high quality, or would you have to borrow one from a friend? In terms of gauging the level of importance, having the camera may be critical, whereas having a reflector for your white light inputs may not be extremely necessary, depending on the content that you'd be shooting. Based on your skills and interests, the most attractive microbusiness opportunity will likely result from the skill and interest area in which you have the most complementary resources. We believe that your resources factor into your ability to execute a specific idea well.

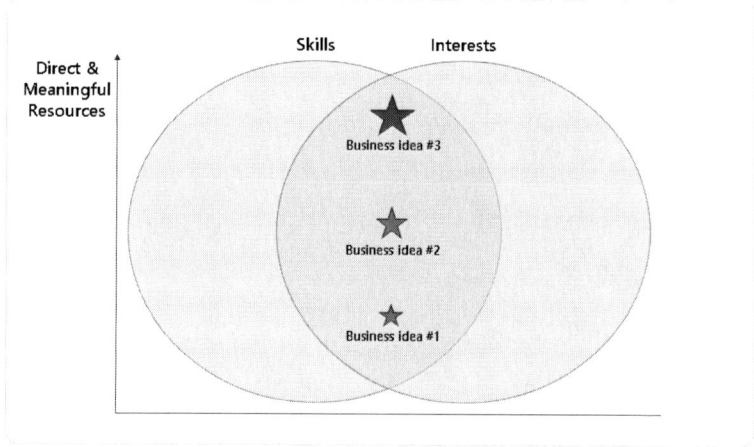

Even if you lack resources, there are things you can do to develop those resources with additional effort, but the point here is to use the resource assessment to gauge difficulty related to your microbusiness launch. For example, if your goal is to have a microbusiness that provides Soccer lessons to interested kids in the neighborhood, it would be much easier to execute if you were good at playing Soccer, enjoyed the game and its intricacies, and had direct access to a public Soccer field nearby. Conversely, you'd have a much harder time if you had great Soccer skill and interest, but lived far away from a space that could be used for training sessions. In the latter example, you would have to work harder and find more creative solutions than if your goals aligned with your skills, interests, and resources. Perhaps you could make videos and still be successful by hosting a webpage, but this method alone wouldn't necessarily maximize your goal of helping the kids in the neighborhood.

Our second method of generating potential business ideas is to go problem-hunting. You can think about problems that you currently have, look into the problems of people you know, or reach out to people in an area of interest to understand more about the problems they face today. Drawing from your own experience, try to find things that create inconvenient moments for you, or from things that you think could be better. When you identify these problems, you can perform research to learn more about them, and try to build out a resolution that is either the first-of-its-kind or better than the current set of proposed solutions. For example, if you've been looking for a particular accessory, but you think the current design lacks the color scheme that you have in mind, you might be able to create that color scheme yourself. How likely is it that other people share the same sentiment? Maybe you've identified a little niche to create a small stream of revenue by being the sole provider of a popular design that your friends really like. I've seen people buy white headphones from a company that offered no alternative color option and pay another company to paint the headphones another color. The companies that offer this recoloring service charge anywhere from ten to twenty percent of the cost of the headphones, and something like this can be executed as a sustainable microbusiness.

When you look for problems to solve, you may find a great opportunity that doesn't necessarily align with your skills and interest. At that point, you can decide whether you want to pursue it or not. If you do pursue an opportunity that falls outside of your skill and interest areas, you can choose to improve your skillset and even bring on a partner with more experience in that space. If the learning curve and partnering approach seems too difficult, you can continue working through your list to find your next opportunity. However, it is possible for you to hit the jackpot by finding a problem in an area where your expertise, interest, and resources intersect. If you find something like this, a solution of yours could be a great business idea, but you'll have to do some research to refine it further.

Step 4 – Initial Refinement of Your Business Ideas

When you've identified one or a few business ideas that you're excited about, what do you do next? Maybe you've found a business idea that solves a problem in an area where you have great skill, interest, and resources, but you shouldn't dive head first just yet. Many people start executing on their initial idea, and they spend a lot of time and money before really asking the core questions that every aspiring founder should ask. To see if you really have an opportunity on your hands, you should perform an initial check by thinking about the answers to the questions below:

- Is this idea satisfying an unmet need? How big is the need?
- Who do you expect to be your core customers and/or target audience?
- How competitive is the space? Who else has a similar offering?
- How would you define success?
- How well does the idea fit with the goals you've identified for yourself?

First things first: Is your idea satisfying an unmet need? This is an extremely important question because if you're solving a non-existent problem, you're not really providing value to the people you want to help. Also, think about the magnitude of the problem you're solving. How big is the problem, and how many people experience the problem? If you've come up with an idea that solves a problem that you personally have, you might be at risk of being the only person who needs that solution. If you mix ten condiments together and create a sauce that you put on your food, the problem could be that there is no commercial sauce available that tastes like yours, but the ugly truth could be that you're the only one who likes that combination. However, this should not discourage you from trying to find a business idea that solves a personal problem. In fact, many great businesses result from people finding a solution to a personal problem and then finding out that many others share the same problem. If you think your solution will only solve a problem for a tiny group of people, that could be okay too, but you should have an idea of this before you get started.

When you're thinking about the problem you're solving, you should be able to hypothesize about who your core customers or target audience will be. We make the distinction between the two because you may have a business where you don't necessarily have paying customers, but you will have a targeted group of people that you interact with regularly. For example, if you created a non-profit in which you took donated electronics and provided it for free to under-privileged teens, then you technically don't have customers because they're not paying, but you would still have to identify them as the core demographic that you serve.

What do you know about the people you intend to serve or sell to? At this step, a general understanding should suffice, but you'll form a deeper understanding when you thoroughly establish your business strategy later on. A good business is always learning how to better serve its customers, and to do that, you need to know who they are. A lot of successful companies even have detailed customer profiles that will intricately describe their typical customer. To further improve their understanding of customers, companies send out surveys and questionnaires to gather additional feedback and context about their shopping patterns. Even though much of that analysis is done after launching the business, it's still great to have preliminary understanding of who your customer will be when you're starting out. Understanding your customer is critical to having a successful business, so it's never too early to learn about them. You can start by answering basic questions and determining age ranges, where they'll be located, and why they'd want to buy or participate in what you're doing.

At this point, you can do a little research to figure out if someone else is trying to solve the same problem. Don't trick yourself into thinking that there must be someone out there smarter who's already trying to take your business idea. Even though things can get pretty competitive and many business ideas have already been tried, there are still many that haven't yet been attempted. And even if you're not necessarily doing something brand new, there could still be potential upside.

Who else is trying to solve the problem? How are they doing it? If you want to have a small tutoring business, and you know that there are two small tutoring centers in your neighborhood, it doesn't necessarily mean that you can't be successful. Maybe the teachers there are older, but your peers would rather receive help from people closer to their age. Maybe they will really like how clearly you communicate and relatable you are. Maybe your advantage is that you can tutor at the school during lunch, while those tutoring centers are far away from the school and only help in the evenings.

As you refine your business idea, it's really important to define success. Of course, you've already identified goals in Step 2, but defining success for your business idea will make sure that you're in alignment with your goals. For example, if you want to have a microbusiness that offers web design services, you'd need to know whether success means reaching a pre-established monetary target, or developing enough web design experience to land a job with a prestigious company. It's also okay to re-evaluate when you're nearing success and even after you've achieved it, but you want to know upfront what you're working towards so that you can execute accordingly. You don't want to put excess effort into a very small goal, and you don't want to fall short with the effort needed to achieve a big one.

When you're defining success for the microbusiness, and thinking about how the idea connects to your overall goals, you can truly figure out whether the idea is good for you. It is totally possible to have a good business idea that doesn't align with what you want for yourself in the future. You may come up with a great business idea that requires a lot of time and effort, and maybe that additional time and effort would distract you from your true goals. Maybe you find a problem, but your skills and resources are not best suited to solve it yourself, and you decide to instead pursue an opportunity that is best aligned with something you can start tomorrow, and something that better accomplishes your personal goals.

Answering these initial questions will help refine your business idea, and give you a better understanding of the problem and the opportunity. As you get a better grasp of the opportunity, you should reflect and see how it compares with other microbusinesses you'd be interested in launching.

Step 5 – Re-evaluating Opportunities

You've come up with a microbusiness idea and you've already refined it. You have a pretty good understanding of what the opportunity is, and you feel like you're ready to dive deeper and create a formal business strategy. Not so fast. What about the other ideas you were thinking about? How are you supposed to gain confidence in the idea you're looking to focus on? Even though your opportunity aligns well with your goals, there may be another idea you have that's even better.

Would it sound crazy if we told you that choosing one idea over another may actually cost you? If one business idea provides you with benefit package A, and an alternative business idea would provide you with benefit package B, you'd technically be giving up benefit package B when you pursue the first idea. However, if benefit package B contained many of the same benefits as package A, and had more total benefits, then you would be happier choosing package B. This concept is known as "opportunity cost," and it helps you understand the cost of choosing one alternative over the other. Luckily, you might not have to forego too much because it's possible to have simultaneous microbusinesses. Just because you have a small tutoring business doesn't mean that you can't sell cookies.

As you re-evaluate your opportunities, if you do find yourself having to choose between several good ideas, don't feel stuck. We all have a limited number of hours each day, and maybe you want to dedicate your time to the one microbusiness idea that will best align with your goals. Be sure to compare your opportunities based on your related skillset, level of interest, and complementary resources, as well as the level of effort required and the overall alignment with your goals. You can even rank each of those areas from one to ten, to see which opportunity gives you the highest total score. Make sure you have a clear understanding of why you're assigning the rankings to those categories. This process should reveal the opportunity that you think is best. Time to move forward and create an official business strategy.

Step 6 – Establishing Business Strategy

As a deeper dive than the initial refinement of your business idea, the establishment of an official business strategy will help you plan exactly how to operate going forward. The business strategy will guide your actions and help you accomplish your microbusiness goals. Even after initially refining the idea, more research must be done as you prepare to launch.

When Weston and I were seniors in college, we studied business cases together to prepare for interviews with consulting firms. In the case studies, you have about thirty to forty minutes to learn about a business problem and recommend strong solutions for a hypothetical company to accomplish their goal. One of the popular approaches that aspiring consultants use to learn more about a particular company is referred to as the **"4C framework."** The four "Cs" stand for Customer, Competition, Capabilities, and Cost. Even though the framework has primarily been used to understand existing businesses, we think it's a great structure for analyzing the key parts of your microbusiness idea.

At the initial refinement stage, you should've answered basic questions about your customer. You've generalized customer age ranges, where they'll be located, and why they'd want to buy or receive your product or service. If we go a little deeper, we can think about different customer types and segmentation. Let's say you want to have a small microbusiness that provides a car washing service in your neighborhood. Maybe you want to be the first to wash the cars, but later on you plan to hire additional staff. In the meantime, you set up a small working station near a popular intersection and attract the eyes of potential customers on their way home from work. You may have a hunch that it's more efficient to establish a central location instead of going door-to-door to wash cars for people who are already home. With this knowledge, you could possibly segment your potential customer base into stationary customers and commuting customers. Are commuting customers more in favor of a quick wash, whereas stationary customers are already home and have time for a more thorough service? Which customer segment presents a bigger opportunity for you? In this example, you might hypothesize that your time would be better spent if you worked at the busy intersection, so maybe you'll start there. During another session, you can try to serve the stationary customers, and see which group works better for you. Segmenting your customer groups enable you to create a better understanding of the demographic you'll be helping. If you understand your potential customer demographics, you'll at least figure out how to start marketing and positioning yourself for success.

We briefly mentioned in the initial refinement step that you should ask general questions about who your competitors are. As you prepare your business strategy, you want to have a more structured approach to understanding exactly which people or organizations are trying to solve the same problem as you. Sticking with the car washing microbusiness example, you'd definitely need to know about the alternatives that your potential customers have to using your service. If there were two automated car wash locations in your area, and 90 percent of your neighbors went there, you might have a really tough time with your microbusiness. This would imply two things: 1) There doesn't seem to be an unmet need for people to get their cars washed, and 2) if they did buy from you, they would need a strong reason to choose your services over the automated service.

The good thing for you is that even though the opportunity doesn't seem huge, you still may be able to succeed. For example, if you donate 30 percent of your car wash earnings to an environmental non-profit organization, and you advertise that business model to your potential customers, they may still prefer to give you their business because of the social cause that you support. If your goal is to positively impact the environment and make decent side income from a microbusiness, this combination could work for you, even with two dominant automated car wash facilities nearby. The donation to a non-profit is just one differentiator, but maybe the people like a very detailed hand wash, and the automated wash leaves the customers unsatisfied because they still have to manually clean the interior. You have to understand your competition, and once you know what they do and how they try to solve the problem that you're addressing, you can see if you should move forward the original way you were thinking or determine if you should make changes to your approach.

When developing your business strategy, you need to understand your capabilities. What can you do? What can you do differently than the current competitors? Would you need to do anything differently? If the demand for tutors is high, but the supply is low in your area, maybe you only need to have a decent level of skill in a particular subject for people to want your services. You can also think back to the skills and resources you've already identified. Do you have access to something that your competitors don't? Maybe you've been tutored in the subject already, and now you have great materials and experience that you can use to be really helpful to the people looking for tutors. If time permits and you have enough motivation, don't be afraid to develop new skills and capabilities to better serve your potential customers.

The first three Cs, Customer, Competition, and Capabilities, have all been qualitative. Now you can use all that information to influence your quantitative assessment. How much will it cost you to operate your microbusiness? Most microbusinesses are low cost because they start out with a very small-scale operation that you experiment with, but some microbusinesses can cost a little bit more than others. Based on your skills and resources, you may be able to spend less time and money than others to get started. For example, if you already have a professional camera, then your initial costs will be much lower than someone who needs to purchase or rent a camera to take high quality photos for customers. Also, if you already know how to use a photo editing software, then you won't have to spend as much time on learning how to improve your finished photo quality, meaning that you saved time compared to someone starting in the photography space without having that skill in the beginning. For this purpose, we urge you to think about cost in terms of time and money.

Financial costs for your microbusiness will vary based on the skills and resources you've already accumulated, and the type of microbusiness you're launching. As you think of your own business idea, try to minimize costs wherever it seems reasonable. Remember, microbusinesses are usually lean in terms of operational costs. If you're selling products or services, you'd want to make sure that the amount you have remaining after subtracting your costs from your revenues align with your goals. If your primary goal is to earn experience with your microbusiness, and you determine that you're happy if your costs are equivalent to your revenues, that's okay too. The point where your revenues equal your costs is referred to as the "break-even" point, and you may be receiving additional non-financial benefit that justifies this outcome.

Thinking about non-financial costs, it would be helpful to consider your estimated time commitment. You can do an upfront assessment and budget a certain number of hours each week to develop a microbusiness, or you can think of how much time you'd have to dedicate to an identified business idea to successfully reach your goals. With this approach, you can better manage yourself and have a more accurate understanding of what a business idea is costing you. When you work for a company, they can calculate how much they have to pay you for your time, but it can be easy to lose the value of your time when you're running your own company because you won't necessarily be paying yourself a wage or salary.

This 4C Framework is great for understanding key aspects of your business strategy. Essentially, the information that you've gathered here should give you all the key inputs for understanding who you'll serve, what you're offering, and how you'll do it. All your analysis should be helping you address the who, what, and how questions that underline your strategy. If you'd like to perform even more analysis for your business strategy, we'd also recommend looking up Michael Porter's "Five Forces" framework, as well as the popular "SWOT" analysis. The "Five Forces" framework helps you analyze your competitive environment, and the "SWOT" analysis helps you evaluate your idea based on its strengths and weaknesses, as well as the opportunities and threats that lie ahead should you choose to move forward. We find the 4C framework to be very helpful for microbusiness development, but all three will prompt you to think more about your strategy to figure out exactly how you want to move forward with your idea.

Step 7 – Initiating Your Microbusiness

Armed with six steps of solid planning and a strong business strategy, you are finally ready to initiate your microbusiness. Again, some microbusinesses have launched without taking these steps, but we're walking you through an approach that maximizes your chances of success. Here's where the rubber meets the road. Now, you get to show yourself what you're capable of. At this point, you should have the utmost confidence that you've done all you can to prepare for success.

If you need to buy, rent, or borrow equipment, software, or anything else to get started, now is the time. What you're doing here is bridging the resource gap and securing your ability to initiate your business idea. This applies to you if your microbusiness requires a camera, a subscription, or anything else that you don't have access to. Once you acquire what you need, you can officially launch. Congrats! You've officially moved forward in a way that many people only dream about. Countless people say they want to be business owners, but very few actually initiate a business plan.

Refer to your business strategy to begin reaching out to potential customers or members of your target demographic. If you plan to tutor, this might be the moment where you actually begin communicating to your peers that you officially offer tutoring services. By word-of-mouth or even by planned advertisement, you should be preparing for people to interact with your products or services. You should be preparing to receive your first customers, to positively impact your target demographic, or do anything else you determined to be your initiation steps. If you're designing custom artwork to sell online, maybe you initiate by buying all your materials and signing up for an account with the platform you'll use to showcase your work.

You have all your guidelines in place around how much time you'll dedicate, how much you plan to spend, and how much you plan to earn. Take ownership of this business idea and see how your people react to it. If the initial response is much different than what you've expected, don't worry because you can always troubleshoot. During this period, the feedback you receive is extremely important. You have to be very attentive and focused on listening to the people you wish to serve. If you have to try very hard to get your first sale or even the first serious inquiry about your offering, there could be simple tweaks or adjustments you can make to have things run smoothly. When you initiate, make sure you ask questions and know what your earliest customers like and dislike. From those answers, you can make decisions to stop doing what they don't like, and doing more of what they like as long as it makes sense for you. More on this in the next chapter.

Step 8 – Validation & Further Refinement

To validate your business idea, the most important questions are, "Is this working the way you anticipated?" and "How are the responses from the people your product or service is interacting with?" If it's not working out, you need to learn why. As Weston and I alluded to, your early customers will provide excellent feedback that can be used to improve your strategy and execution. If you're selling cookies, and your first customers are independently letting you know that you need to take it easy on the chocolate chip-to-cookie dough ratio, at least you have the information to determine whether you want to make adjustments to improve the experience of those customers or target people who love very chocolatey cookies.

Speaking of snacks, Weston started a snack-based microbusiness in junior high school. He sold snacks from his locker and eventually earned more daily revenue than the school's vending machines. At his peak, his regular customers included school faculty members, and he even had a loyalty-reward program. They'd buy goods from him on a daily basis and receive discounted rates. He was the vendor of choice on campus, and his breakthrough success came as a result of a few swift adjustments early on.

Before starting his microbusiness, Weston had been known as the kid to ask for gum. He always had it. The demand was high, and Weston was tired of either having to give away free pieces or turn students down. If he gave a piece to every student that asked, he wouldn't have had any left for himself. Here is where he saw the opportunity. He started charging students for the pieces that he was carrying, and when he sold out, he'd tell students he had more in his locker if they met him during break. Every break, students knew where to go to get their gum. He would buy in bulk at the start of each week, and even at $.10 each, he was building out a decent microbusiness for himself. He quickly expanded his offering to sell full packs and different types of gum. After about a month, the Vice Principal pulled Weston aside and told him that he had to stop selling gum because the students kept sticking it on the underside of tables and chairs. This was an outcome that he didn't anticipate, and his locker shop was officially shut down for a week.

Understanding that vandalism was the reason he was being shut down, he figured that he should still be able to operate if he stopped selling gum, and instead sold chips and candy bars. Weston already had students looking forward to stopping by his locker during breaks, and he figured it wouldn't be too hard to sell different snacks to the same people. By buying in bulk, he bought what he anticipated to be about two weeks of inventory, and was able to minimize his cost per item. On his first day as a chip and candy bar, he sold out immediately, and actually wished he brought more snacks from home. He went on to operate this locker shop for over a year-and-a-half, and his lineup grew to even include cold Frappuccino drinks.

Let's take a look at what happened in this example. Weston had initiated his idea to begin selling gum, and was validating how it would play out in the school. The students liked buying gum from him, but the school's regulation proved that selling gum was not sustainable. He had validated the idea of selling snacks to his peers from his locker, but he had to refine his offering. After he quickly made the adjustment, the school staff appreciated his compliance and entrepreneurial approach, and even supported him by purchasing snacks.

In your own microbusiness, don't be surprised if you have to make a few tweaks in the beginning. No one has all the answers. After you launch, you're paying attention to the direct feedback and learning about the adjustments you may need to make to achieve your goal. Aim to validate your strategy and make any necessary refinements.

Step 9 — Execute

The execution phase is great. It means that you've validated your business strategy and made any necessary tweaks to arrive at a point where you can continue to provide value to your customers or target audience. You've refined your approach and now you have something that should continue to help you accomplish your goals. This phase is when you know that your approach actually works. Using Weston's snack locker example, the execution phase is where he sells his snacks and continues to be the reliable vendor that his peers are expecting him to be. He is refreshing his inventory as often as he needs to, and his operation is sustainable.

For entrepreneurs, reaching this stage means that you had a great strategy, made great adjustments, or both. Of course, you're still learning during this phase, and you're getting better at doing what you do. Maybe your car wash microbusiness has helped you find an inter-section that works well for you and generates consistent revenue from noon to 3p.m. on Sundays, so you go there every Sunday. If you have a tutoring microbusiness and due to time constraints, you plan on only helping two students during the semester, and you already have two student clients, then maybe you wouldn't have to dedicate time towards finding new students during the execution phase. The time that you save from not having to promote your services can be spent elsewhere. You have an efficient operation. At this point, you could probably sustainably tutor those two students without making strategic adjustments. You know your customer, competition, capa-bilities, and cost, and you feel confident that the continuation of this microbusiness will lead you to your goal.

Step 10 – Determine Next Steps

If your microbusiness has successfully made it to the execution phase, Congratulations! Now, you have a really great choice to make. You can either choose to maintain operations to achieve your anticipated results, or you can make the decision to scale to either accomplish your goal faster or exceed your original goal. Let's revisit the Building BLOC case study. If you remember, Building BLOC had already been meeting the goal that Weston and I set out to achieve. We wanted to create a non-profit that would allow us to help high school students with college and career development. We were only helping one high school, but we were providing mentorship and guidance, and the experience was deeply fulfilling. Maintaining this level of service would have been great, but the success of our second microbusiness gave us an opportunity to expand Building BLOC's offering to a national level. There was no pressure to expand nationally, but Weston and I made the choice to scale because we really enjoyed the type of work and the positive impact that we were creating.

At this phase, reflection is key. We put together a list of questions you can ask yourself to figure out your next steps:

- Do you enjoy running your microbusiness? What are your likes and dislikes?
- Would you enjoy doing more of it than you originally intended?
- Do you see an opportunity to expand or scale?
- Have your goals changed since you began? If so, how?

Even at a young age, microbusinesses enable you to test ideas and practice entrepreneurship, and because it's not something you absolutely have to do, we hope that you enjoy the process and the overall experience. If you're running a microbusiness that you no longer enjoy, that's okay, but the quicker you understand what changed and what your dislikes are, the quicker you'll be able to make the necessary adjustments to get a better outcome. Should you make a few tweaks to the way you're doing business, or should you pursue another idea altogether? With reasons ranging from business operation being a bigger-than-expected time commitment to just wanting to try something different in your free time, you have to be self-aware and ask yourself how much you enjoy the microbusiness experience. For those that really enjoy it, the process is fun, and each obstacle presents an opportunity to problem-solve and create new solutions. If you do enjoy running a microbusiness, would you enjoy putting more into it, or would additional hours make it feel like more of an obligation?

While executing your microbusiness, you may identify opportunities to expand or scale. Usually, when you scale, it involves serving new customers, increasing your offering, or becoming a larger company with more staff. If you have a microbusiness where you rent out your clothes, maybe there's an opportunity to buy more of the "high-in-demand" clothing to increase your rental volume and revenue. You want to stay sharp and understand the trends that are happening in your business space, and if you practice the ability to identify opportunity, it will serve you forever. Also, just because you see an opportunity to expand or scale, doesn't necessarily mean that you should. Maybe you see something new that you can sell to a customer base that would love to buy it from you, but if the investment cost is too high or the complexity is too much at the time, you can choose to pass on that specific opportunity.

You should also check in with yourself to see if your goals are unchanged from before you started the microbusiness. If you originally wanted to be a social media influencer in the fashion industry, but after deep reflection you think you'd most enjoy a career training pets, your microbusiness execution may have to change. Even if you're executing a microbusiness and it seems like you'd be able to maintain it in a relatively easy manner, always be aware of how the microbusiness is helping you accomplish the goals that you've identified in Step 2.

10-Step Roadmap: Conclusion

We have now walked you through the 10-step approach you should take to launch and sustainably operate a microbusiness. The first step was to decide whether you'd actually want to pursue entrepreneurship and gain microbusiness experience. After learning about microbusinesses and understanding that you can often get started with very little cost, it's important for you to strive toward being a successful microbusiness owner. Next, you identify detailed goals and formulate business ideas that can help you achieve those goals. Then, you filter those business ideas, find one that best aligns with your skills, interests, and resources, and develop it further by establishing an official business strategy. After your business strategy is set, launch your microbusiness and closely listen to the initial feedback. Lastly, try to validate and refine your microbusiness operation to the point where you can choose to maintain a good operation at its current growth rate, or scale further.

If you decide to scale your microbusiness and grow, you could potentially create a large company, depending on the size of the opportunity. However, additional scaling usually requires more time and money, and could require you to bring on partners or additional employees to meet your business needs. If your microbusiness grows from a two-person team to a group of forty employees, it's safe to say you may no longer be a running microbusiness. Even though running a microbusiness will help you develop amazing skills, if you keep increasing the size of your operation, you'll definitely reach a point where you'll be required to acquire additional skills and capabilities, especially if you're managing other people. Who knows, maybe your microbusiness will transition to becoming a startup, and even a publicly listed company on the New York Stock Exchange. Or maybe your microbusiness becomes a non-profit organization that solves a universal problem by helping to protect and preserve eco-systems around the world. Either way, always keep your goals in mind and understand how your microbusiness is helping you achieve the broader goals that you identified in Step 2.

It's also important to note that at any step, you can always revisit an earlier point in the roadmap. For example, if you're estab-lishing the business strategy for an idea that you're really interested in, and your research finds that the competition is too strong, you can go back and re-evaluate your other opportunities to see if another idea seems more attractive. If you've re-evaluated your business ideas, and you find no interest pursuing any of the remaining options, you can go back to Step 3 and formulate new ideas. During your microbusiness journey, you'll always be learning and reflecting, so thinking about how new information might impact the execution of your idea is always warranted.

Overall, these ten steps represent the key components of cre-ating a microbusiness that will help you successfully accomplish your goals. If you follow these steps, your microbusiness should be much more sustainable and fully aligned with the future you see for yourself.

PART IV:
CLOSING THOUGHTS

"You never lose in business. Either you WIN or you LEARN."

-Melinda Emerson

First and foremost, thank you for taking the time to read our book. There are many books and articles out there to help people grow their businesses, but we saw that there didn't seem to be much guidance on how teens and young adults can get early experience and initiate low-risk business ideas. In this book, we've done three things: Defined what a microbusiness is, performed a detailed review of microbusiness case studies, and shared a roadmap for you to plan, launch, and execute your own microbusiness.

Whether you launch several microbusinesses like Warren Buffett in his childhood, or only initiate a single experience, we think that you'll be able to have fun and work toward your goals, while learning first-hand how to run your own operation. At the very least, the experience should help you figure out if being a business owner is a path you want to take. There are plenty of ways to have a successful career without being a business owner, but at least you can gain an early understanding of how things work. Even if you decide that you don't necessarily want to have a sophisticated business right now, maybe you'll learn things that will help you when you're ready later on.

If you have a side hustle right now and you have entrepreneurial aspirations, we hope that we've inspired you to look for additional opportunities to create a business operation that is better aligned with the holistic goals you've established for yourself. The distinction between a side hustle and a microbusiness is determined by the individual's primary intention, and with the right mindset, you can try to find opportunities to scale your side hustle into a microbusiness.

If you do pursue your own microbusiness, we genuinely hope that you are fulfilled by the experience. There's something truly exciting about creating a system or organization that didn't exist before your idea came around, no matter how small. Don't worry about the size of your initial microbusiness. A small step in the right direction is much better than doing nothing. There are always small steps we can take to help us reach our goals, and after a while, even your distant goals become within reach. If you do want to be a successful business owner, launching and operating your own microbusiness is an amazing small step you can take. Over time, your knowledge will compound and you'll be a great business leader.

Also, while we do encourage you to pursue entrepreneurship, this book did not explain the intricacies of filing federal and state taxes for earned income. To address this, we advise that you research the filing protocol within your geography and age range to understand your compliance needs.

Lastly, if reading this book inspires you to launch and operate a microbusiness, please let us know by sending an email to

KhiryKemp@gmail.com. We are deeply passionate about helping teens and young adults pursue entrepreneurship, and we'd love to hear about your attempts and early success. We believe that you're all capable of changing the world, and we're excited to see where your microbusinesses take you. Embrace the journey, gain business experience, and don't forget to have fun!